George Washington

Dona Herweck

D0008544

Consultant

Timothy Rasinski, Ph.D.
Kent State University

Publishing Credits

Dona Herweck Rice, *Editor-in-Chief*
Robin Erickson, *Production Director*
Lee Aucoin, *Creative Director*
Conni Medina, M.A.Ed., *Editorial Director*
Jamey Acosta, *Editor*
Stephanie Reid, *Photo Editor*
Rachelle Cracchiolo, M.S.Ed., *Publisher*

Image Credits
Cover ullstein bild/The Granger Collection; p.2 Studio_G/Shutterstock; p.3 fckncg/ Shutterstock; p.4 left: Peter Wey/Shutterstock; p.4 right: Reinhold Leitner/Shutterstock; p.5 AVprophoto/Shutterstock; p.6 LC-DIG-pga-03120; p.7 top: LC-DIG-pga-01368; p.7 inset: Kate Connes/Shutterstock; p.8 The Granger Collection, New York; p.9 The Granger Collection, New York; p.10 top: fckncg/Shutterstock; p.10 bottom: Historical Picture Archive/CORBIS; p.11 The Granger Collection, New York; p.12 The Granger Collection, New York; p.13 Album/Prisma/ Newscom; p.14-15 The Granger Collection, New York; p.15 top: LC-DIG-pga-02417; p.15 inset: The Granger Collection, New York; p.16 LC-DIG-pga-02419; p.17 top: LC-USZ62-49921; p.17 inset: LC-H8-CT-M04-009; p.18 top: The Granger Collection, New York; p.18 bottom: Kasia/Shutterstock; p.19 LC-DIG-ds-00123; p.20-21 The Granger Collection, New York; p.21 LC-USZC2-3154; p.22 LC-USZC2-3793; p.23 LC-USZC2-3310; p.24 LC-USZ62-117747; p.24-25 LC-USZC4-12011; p.26 LC-D4-32091; p.27 top to bottom: The Granger Collection, New York; LC-DIG-pga-02417; LC-USZC2-3793; LC-USZC4-12011; back cover Kasia/Shutterstock

Based on writing from *TIME For Kids*.

TIME For Kids and the *TIME For Kids* logo are registered trademarks of TIME Inc. Used under license.

Teacher Created Materials

5301 Oceanus Drive
Huntington Beach, CA 92649-1030
http://www.tcmpub.com

ISBN 978-1-4333-3640-9

© 2012 Teacher Created Materials, Inc.
Made in China
Nordica.092015.CA21501360

Table of Contents

The Cherry Tree

Young George had a new axe that he couldn't wait to use. The shiny metal was sharp and the wooden handle was smooth and glossy. George's parents thought he was ready to have an axe of his own. They knew they could trust their honest son to use it wisely.

Most of the time George made good choices about what to do. But now he wasn't thinking. He felt he would burst if he didn't try using the axe. It was then that he saw the cherry tree.

George's father had just planted the tree. But George didn't think about that. The young tree was just the right size for chopping, and that is just what George did. He chopped down the cherry tree.

George knew right away that it was wrong. He was ashamed. So he bravely walked to his father and said, "Father, I cannot tell a lie. I chopped down the cherry tree."

Did this really happen? No, but people like to tell the story anyway. It shows that George was an honest and brave person.

Do you know who George grew up to be? He was George Washington, the first **president** of the United States of America.

Early Life

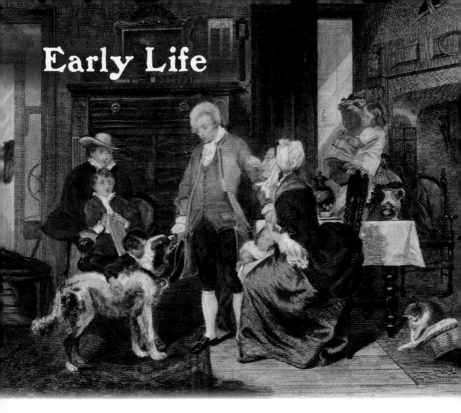

George Washington was born in Virginia on February 22, 1732. At that time, all of America belonged to England.

George's parents, Augustine and Mary, were wealthy farmers. George's father died when George was 11, so his older half-brother, Lawrence, helped to raise him.

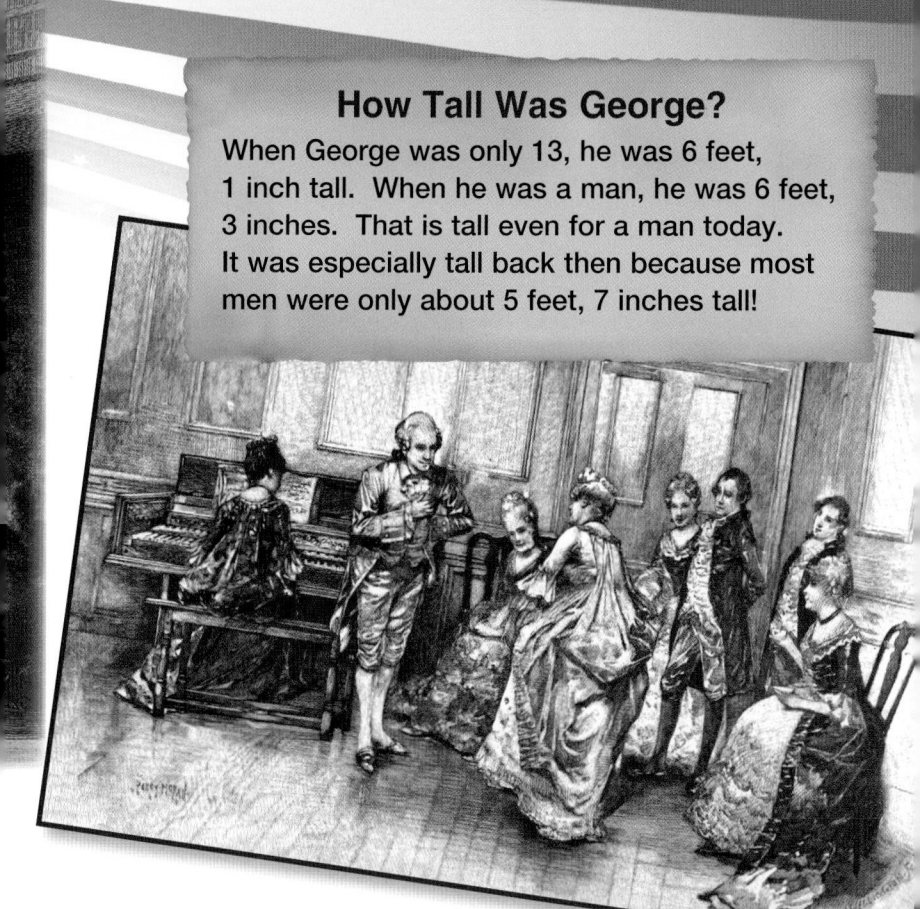

How Tall Was George?

When George was only 13, he was 6 feet, 1 inch tall. When he was a man, he was 6 feet, 3 inches. That is tall even for a man today. It was especially tall back then because most men were only about 5 feet, 7 inches tall!

George was a bright boy who especially liked math. He was tall and strong and liked to be active outdoors. As he grew older, George enjoyed music and going to the theater. He also liked to dance, but he was shy around girls.

A Life at Sea

George really wanted to be a seaman and live on the water. His mother gave him permission, and George was ready to go. But at the last minute she changed her mind. She would not allow George to leave home and go to sea. She was very strict, and George had to obey. He gave up that dream for good and turned to surveying instead.

George enjoyed many things. But the most important thing to him was to do well. He wanted to gain wealth and respect. So, George worked hard.

Surveyor

What is a surveyor? A surveyor measures land and all its hills and valleys. The measurements are used in maps and to help people know where to build. Surveying is a type of math. George's math skills helped him to be a good surveyor.

George studied and traveled with Lawrence. He learned a lot from him. George used his knowledge to become a **surveyor** (ser-VEY-er) when he was only 17.

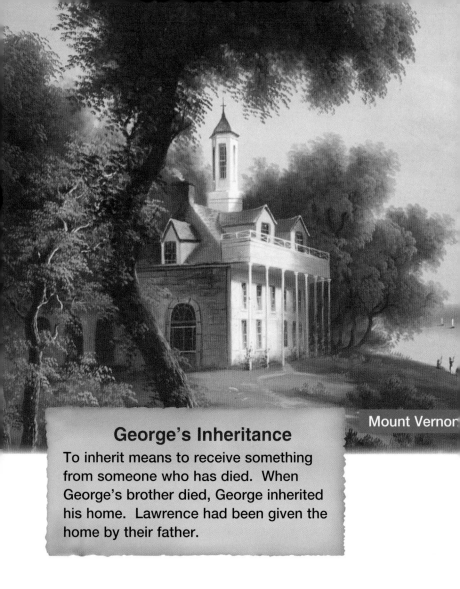

Mount Vernon

George's Inheritance

To inherit means to receive something from someone who has died. When George's brother died, George inherited his home. Lawrence had been given the home by their father.

When George was 20, Lawrence died. George **inherited** Mount Vernon, one of the Washington family **plantations**.

Militia

A militia is like an army that is called to duty during emergencies. Today we call such groups the National Guard or the Army Reserves. Military describes things that are related to armies and soldiers.

George was also given his brother's job. Lawrence was an officer in the Virginia **militia** (mi-LISH-uh). Even though George was only 20 and had no army experience, he knew he could do the job. This was the start of his **military** (MIL-i-ter-ee) career.

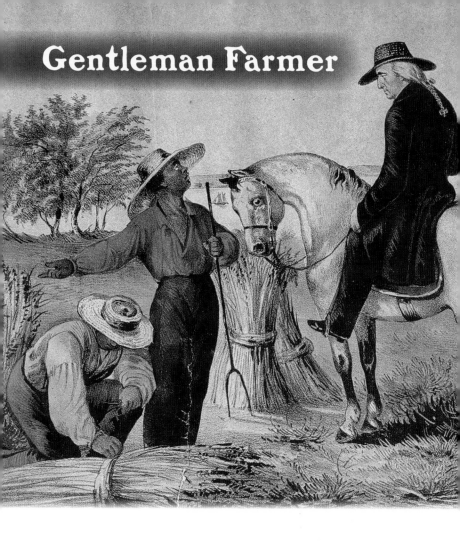

Gentleman Farmer

George was a military leader until his late twenties. Then he thought his work was finished. He returned to Mount Vernon, Virginia, to farm the land.

My Dear Patsy

George did not call his wife Martha. When she was a young girl, she was called Patsy. She liked that name best. So, George called her "my dear Patsy."

In 1759, George married Martha Dandridge Custis. She was a wealthy **widow** with two children, Jacky and Patsy. George became their stepfather.

George was a good farmer. He read everything he could about farming. He tried new and better ways to farm.

To improve his plantation, he set up **fisheries**, a **mill**, and an **ironworks**.

Plantation Businesses

George had many businesses! A fishery is a special place for hatching and catching fish. A mill grinds wheat and other grains and turns them into flour. An ironworks is a place where workers can make things and build with iron. George used all of these to help him on his plantation. They made his plantation more successful.

mill at Mount Vernon

slaves working in a fishery

George became a leader among his neighbors. He was such a strong leader that he became part of Virginia's **government**. For 15 years, he helped to make laws there.

Temper, Temper

George was known for his fierce temper. He had promised his father that he would not let his temper control him. He always worked hard to stay calm and keep his head clear. Doing this helped him to be a good leader.

Revolution!

Baron Friedrich von Steuben trains American revolutionary soliders.

Things started to change in America. Many people living in America thought England was unfair to them. They wanted to have their own country.

Washington is appointed as commander-in-chief.

George got the militia ready for war. In 1775, he was named commander of the new American army.

The fighting was long and hard, and many people died. One winter in Valley Forge, Pennsylvania, George and his army barely survived. They were cold and had little food, but they made it.

Father of Our Country

Many people believe that if not for George, the new country might not have lasted. There were many different ideas and disagreements. George worked hard to keep people together. That is why he is called the "Father of Our Country."

Finally, after eight long years of war, peace was declared in 1783. American leaders agreed to form a new country and call it the United States of America.

George went home, but not forever. The country needed a new leader. The leader would be called President of the United States. They thought George was right for the job.

George knew it was an important job. He was afraid to make mistakes, but he took the job and worked hard for the new country. He listened to what the people wanted.

George was president for eight years. He thought that was long enough. He told the people it was time for a new president. They elected John Adams. In 1797, George finally went home to Virginia.

Washington arrives in Philadelphia for his second inauguration in 1793.

Back Home Again

George was glad to be home with his family. He helped the new country when he could, but mainly he stayed home.

On December 14, 1799, George woke up feeling ill. Later that night, he died.

George had been a great leader and will always be remembered. One friend said it best. He said that George was "first in war, first in peace, and first in the hearts of his countrymen."

Washington Time Line

1732	born in Virginia on February 22
1749	became a surveyor ••••••••••••••
1752	• Lawrence's death • inheritance of Mt. Vernon • appointment to the militia
1759	• married to Martha Dandridge Custis ••• • member of the Virginia House of Burgesses from 1759 to 1774
1774	• elected to the First Continental Congress • organized militia from 1774 to 1775
1775	• named general and commander-in-chief of the American army on June 15 • American Revolution begins from 1775 to 1783 ••••••••••••••••••••••••
1776	signing of the Declaration of Independence on July 4
1787	signing of the United States Constitution on September 17
1789	elected President of the United States on February 4
1792	re-elected President of the United States ••••••••••••••••••••••
1799	died at Mt. Vernon on December 14

Glossary

fisheries—special places for hatching and catching fish

government—groups of people who make the laws and are in charge of all the people and their protection

inherited—received by legal right from a person at the person's death

ironworks—a place where workers make and build with iron

military—describes things that are related to armies and soldiers

militia—an army that is called to duty during emergencies

mill—a place to grind grain and turn it into flour

plantations—very large farms with many crops and workers

president—the highest officer in a group

surveyor—a person who measures land and all its hills and valleys

widow—a man or a woman whose wife or husband has died